This Study Belongs To

Start Date

/ /

WOMEN OF JOY

loved

an eight week study

Debbie & Phil Waldrep

Debbie & Phil Waldrep

At Women of Joy, we seek to make an eternal difference in the life of every person. The speakers, musicians and special guests all share in our aim.

While many wonderful things happen at these events, there is nothing like the lasting impact of studying God's Word. It comforts us, challenges us and convicts us.

This "LOVED" Bible study explores the conversations women had with Jesus and draws a direct connection between their interactions and your own personal relationship with Christ.

We encourage you to find a quiet place, get your Bible and a pen, and ask our Heavenly Father to speak to you as you spend eight weeks in the shoes of the women who came face-to-face with Jesus and discovered first hand that they were loved.

Please know that we are praying for you as you study. We agree with the Apostle Paul when he wrote in Philippians 1:6, "And I am sure of this, that he who began a good work in you will bring it to completion at the day of Jesus Christ."

Debbie and Phil Waldrep
Co-founders & Directors
Women of Joy

Debbie + Phil

Table of Contents

You Are Loved!

"Mary therefore took a pound of expensive ointment made from pure nard, and anointed the feet of Jesus and wiped his feet with her hair. The house was filled with the fragrance of the perfume."

John 12:3

It is one of the most emotionally moving moments recorded in the Gospel of John. Jesus was the guest of honor at a dinner in Bethany. After eating, He was relaxing when Mary brought an expensive ointment and anointed his feet. Then, she took her hair and wiped the excess away (John 12:1-3). To everyone watching, it was an act of deep and sincere love.

We could understand Mary's actions if she was a servant following orders from her boss. Or if she was trying to outdo her sister, Martha, who just prepared the wonderful meal they consumed. But Mary's actions were out of the ordinary.

Mary was outwardly expressing her gratitude for the way Jesus valued her as a woman who, by societal standards, should be ignored. Jesus loved Mary unconditionally.
Think, for a moment, of the ways Mary knew that Jesus loved her.

When He came for visits to their home, Jesus listened to her thoughts and ideas. Her feelings and her insights mattered to Him. Jesus probably asked her thoughts about life, politics, and spiritual issues. Jesus valued her opinion because He valued her.

On one occasion, Mary's sister, Martha, criticized her in the presence of Jesus (Luke 10:40-42). Jesus defended Mary quickly. Martha's words probably hurt Mary, but Jesus came to her rescue.

Mary, Martha and Lazarus were siblings who lived together. They were a close family. When Lazarus died, grief overwhelmed Mary. She didn't want to leave her home.

But when Jesus arrived and asked for her, Mary went to Him. She was weeping and broken. And when Jesus saw her weeping, He wept (John 11:35).

Later, Jesus would raise Lazarus from the dead, but for a few moments Jesus felt what Mary was feeling.

Jesus loved Mary.

Jesus made her feel alive, and He brought out the best in her.

Mary knew Jesus didn't want anything from her. He wasn't seeking a romantic relationship or trying to manipulate her to satisfy His own wishes.

Jesus loved and valued her because of who she was.

1. **Take a moment to think of the times when you felt loved unconditionally by someone. Make a list of the things these people did/said that caused you to feel that way.**

Daron loving me for who I am.
Vicki going to counseling
Vicki being there when my anxiety so bad.

Love is a word often used to describe something we like. (For example, you might hear someone say, "I love ice cream.") But love is more than liking something or someone.

Love implies a relationship. It is caring about the well-being of another person. It implies respect.

2. **Read I Corinthians 13:4-7. Using these verses as a guide, circle the following sentences that are true:**

Love is kind.	Love is resentful.
Love is selfish.	Love is patient.
Love is arrogant.	Love is forgiving

Before Christ was born, the society in Palestine didn't value women. Every man in power pushed women to the sidelines.

Socially, the Romans who ruled the region didn't accept women as equal to men, especially in government affairs.

The Jewish leaders prayed and thanked God every day that they weren't born a Gentile, a slave or a woman. Even the pagans didn't respect women beyond their child-bearing roles.

Women had to find their "dignity" in the men in their lives – their fathers, their husbands or their sons.

As a result, widows often became homeless and begged for food. Women who could not bear children were viewed as cursed by God. And no man, outside of their immediate family, cared if they lived or died.

And into this world stepped Jesus.

In this study we will examine the conversations and interactions women had with Jesus. We will see how Jesus saw them as valuable to God and how He was willing to challenge the social norms to prove it. By His words and His actions, Jesus elevated the dignity of women and loved them unconditionally.

Best of all, we will see how Jesus views you the same way!

3 **What are some things you hope you see and learn from these interactions between Jesus and women? List them here.**

1. ______________________________

2. ______________________________

3. ______________________________

Week One

1

You Are Loved :
WHEN YOU ARE CALLED TO A PURPOSE

"And he came to her and said, "Greetings, O favored one, the Lord is with you!"

Luke 1:28

Have you ever been going through your day when something wonderful happened? Suddenly, you learned you are getting a raise from your employer, the house you have been trying to sell gets a good offer, your child gets accepted into a prestigious college or you win a fabulous family vacation.

Everyone loves a nice surprise!

But what about spiritual surprises? You know, the ones where God chooses you or calls you to a specific purpose? Whether it is a special moment and place when your Lord speaks clearly about what He is wanting you to do, or something you realize over time, how do you respond?

1 **Is there something you know God called you to do? Or is there something you think God might be calling you to do? It doesn't have to be on a grand scale or involve lots of people. It could involve just one person. If so, write about your calling here.**

One of the women in the New Testament that received an assignment from God was Mary, the mother of Jesus. Mary was present throughout the life of Jesus and in the early days of the church.

2 **People mention Mary at Christmas but rarely see the other times she interacted with Jesus and believers. Look up each of these Scriptures and write the places and events where Mary was present and what she did.**

Luke 2:6-7:

Luke 2:41-51:

John 2:1-12:

John 19:26-27:

Acts 1:14:

Mary received one assignment from her Heavenly Father: she was to birth and rear the Son of God! He loved her so much that He entrusted her with this great honor that no other woman would ever experience.

The gospel writer Luke gave us the details of the day she received her calling.

Mary was having a routine day when the angel Gabriel appeared. Fear gripped her heart. Since some Jewish leaders taught that death followed an encounter with an angel, Mary had a reason to be afraid.

Gabriel eliminated her fear by saying, "Do not be afraid, Mary, for you have found favor with God" (Luke 1:30). The phrase "found favor" often is translated "highly favored" or "greatly graced."

Mary did not come from a prominent family. In fact, she was poor. According to Luke 2:24 and Leviticus 12:8, the offering Mary and Joseph offered at the circumcision of Jesus indicated their poverty. She possessed no special talents or personal charisma. She was an ordinary young woman who loved God. It was God's grace, or favor, that chose her.

3 **When God gives someone an assignment, He often chooses a common person without any special skill for the calling. Read I Corinthians 1:26-29. Using verse 29 as your guide, complete this sentence:**

God uses ordinary people "so that ____________________ might boast in the ____________________ of God."

Like anyone fulfilling God's mission for her life, Mary faced challenges. Questions surely went through her mind: What if her fiancé and family members didn't believe her? How would she deal with the negative comments from others? Yet, Mary submitted herself to God's plan for her life.

Slowly, Mary began to see God work. An angel clarified things for Joseph (Matt. 1:20-21). Then the Lord brought someone into her life to encourage her.

Gabriel told Mary that an older relative, Elizabeth, had conceived a child. Mary went to visit her for three months. During that time, Elizabeth affirmed her and joined her in praising God.

4 **When God gives you a mission, it is important to receive wise counsel and encouragement from others. It is vital when you are finding and fulfilling your calling. Who has God placed in your life to encourage and advise you? What do they do that affirms your calling? Write your answer here. Think about copying it later in a personal note and send to your encourager.**

After the birth of Jesus, Mary was a faithful wife and mother. When Jesus was 12, the family went to Jerusalem for the annual Passover. Families traveled in caravans for safety and convenience. It wasn't unusual for children to be with another family in the group as they traveled.

When they left Jerusalem, Mary and Joseph assumed Jesus was with some boys from another family. That night, after traveling a whole day, Mary and Joseph realized Jesus was missing.

The next day they returned to Jerusalem. Three days later they found Jesus in the Temple talking with the religious leaders. Sure, Mary expressed her displeasure with Jesus, but Jesus reminded her of His purpose and, in doing so, of her calling as well (Luke 2:41-51).

When God calls you to a purpose, assuming can be dangerous. Mary assumed Jesus was with the caravan. Believers often assume God is going to act in a certain way because He called us, but you must be responsible and prepared for all the things God entrusted to you.

5 **Listed below are four things Christians often fail to do. How does each failure indicate that the Christian may be assuming something about their spiritual life?**

Failing to read the Bible

Failing to pray

Failing to attend church

Failing to give

Mary was uncertain of God's plan, but she patiently waited for the time when Jesus would reveal to the world who He was.

One of the most difficult seasons in a Christian's life is the time between knowing their calling and fulfilling it. Often, God uses this time to mature us for the role.

6 **Maturity comes from listening and learning. Often, learning comes through good and bad experiences. What is one experience that grew you spiritually? What three things did you learn from it?**

When Jesus began His earthly ministry, He immediately called His first six disciples. Shortly thereafter, Jesus and these disciples joined His mother, Mary, at a wedding (John 2:1-12).

Weddings were events that lasted seven days. The groom and his family furnished the food for the attendees all week. Nothing was more embarrassing than for the groom to run out of food!

The groom's family probably were friends of Mary. In fact, she may have assisted with the meals. When they ran out of wine, Mary told the servants to obey whatever Jesus told them.

Mary knew Jesus was the promised Messiah. She was anxious for everyone else to know. The tone of her actions indicate that she wanted Jesus to reveal who He was.

Jesus politely reminded his mother that God's schedule wasn't her schedule. He knew that patience is necessary when God calls you.

7

Patience is hard when you have a calling or a mission from God. We want to rush the process. In each of the following things, what happens when you lack patience and try to rush the process?

Baking a cake

Driving across town

Perfecting a sport

Growing as a Christian

Even when our calling is clear, it sometimes doesn't develop the way we thought. God occasionally takes us in a different direction than we anticipated.

Can you imagine how Mary felt, knowing Jesus was the promised Messiah, when He was crucified? Fortunately, Mary's sister and some friends were with her at the cross (John 19:25).

Jesus loved Mary. He knew that she did not understand what was happening and why. On the cross, He assigned his disciple, John, to care for Mary the rest of her life (John 19:26-27).

8 **When you sense that your dream died, or the calling that was clear may not happen, how do you react? Abraham in the Old Testament had a calling from God. Read Romans 4:20-21. Using your Bible, complete the following sentences that show how Abraham reacted.**

"No distrust made him ____________________ concerning the ____________________ of God, but he grew strong in his ____________________ as he gave glory to God, fully convinced that God was able to do what he had ____________________ ."

The resurrection of Jesus validated what God told Mary. She saw the completion of her calling. God kept His Word!

9 **Read again your response to the first question in this section – the one where you wrote what God has called you to do. After examining Mary's life, how do you plan to respond?**

Further Study

Some people struggle with finding their purpose. One of the ways is examining your passions (interests) and your spiritual gifts. God equipped you and gave you a passion to see something accomplished. Read Romans 12:3-8 and make a list of the spiritual gifts mentioned. Which gift(s) do you think you possess? How can you use your gift and your passion to find your purpose?

Journal your Journey

Prayer Requests

Week Two

2

You Are Loved :
WHEN OTHERS JUDGE YOUR SIN

"And Jesus said, 'Neither do I condemn you; go, and from now on sin no more.'"

John 8:11b

Do you remember the novel you probably read in high school entitled The Scarlet Letter by Nathaniel Hawthorne? Set in the Puritan Massachusetts Bay Colony, it tells the fictitious story of Hester Prynne, a woman who gave birth to a child while unmarried. She is forced to wear a scarlet "A" on her chest to remind her and others of her sin.

The father of the child, however, remains unknown until the end of the book. The minister of her church, Arthur Dimmesdale, who participated in publicly shaming her, finally admits that he is the father.

Many believers often feel they are wearing a letter that identifies their sin. Whether true or not, they think everyone is shaming and judging them.

Although they have confessed and turned from their sin, they continue to feel guilt and shame.

1 Look at the list of people below. Circle the ones that may struggle with thinking people are shaming them for their sin.

Unwed mother	Pastor
Godly Bible Teacher	Divorced Person
Former Drug Addict	Beauty Contest Winner

It might surprise you to know that all the ones listed above might be feeling shame and rejection from other Christians. Some wrongs are public, but others are known only to a few. Both groups, however, might feel an embarrassment from the past.

Shame isolates us. It affects relationships. It forces us to wonder if someone will like us or accept us "if they knew." It makes us feel alone.

The Gospel of John records the story of an unnamed woman who experienced the judgment, shame and rejection of religious people.

Jesus went with his disciples to the Feast of Tabernacles in Jerusalem. While He was there, Jesus began teaching in the Temple. His teachings prompted the Pharisees to openly criticize and debate Him. The Pharisees were trying to trick Jesus into saying or doing something that would allow them to arrest Him.

One morning Jesus was teaching in an area of the Temple known as the Court of Women. It was one of the few areas where women could go. As Jesus taught, the Pharisees brought a woman they caught in a sexual act with a man that wasn't her husband and forced her to sit in the middle of the crowd (John 8:2-4).

It probably was a set-up. They obviously knew where she was and knew when to arrive to catch her.

2 **Judgmental people often draw attention to a person's sin by their actions. On a scale of 1-10 with 1 being never and 10 being often, how regularly do you feel one of these has happened to you?**

People staring	1	2	3	4	5	6	7	8	9	10
Whispering as you walk by	1	2	3	4	5	6	7	8	9	10
Gossiping about you	1	2	3	4	5	6	7	8	9	10
Avoiding you	1	2	3	4	5	6	7	8	9	10

Judgmental people tend to be selective and inconsistent with their standards. For example, the man involved in the adultery wasn't present. The Law required stoning of both the man and the woman caught in adultery (Leviticus 20:10).

Was he a friend or relative of the Pharisees? Did the man know something about the accusers? Was he an influential leader? Maybe a Roman soldier that could cause problems for the Jewish leaders?

The motive of the Pharisees was clear: they wanted to trick Jesus into saying something that would turn people against Him.

When the Pharisees asked if they should stone her as the Law required, they thought that Jesus was in a bind. If Jesus said that they should stone her, his popularity would decrease rapidly. If Jesus said that they should not, He gave them grounds for accusing Him of disobeying the Law. To the judgmental Pharisees, they won regardless of Jesus' answer.

3 **Jesus warned about the consequences of judging others. Read Luke 6:37. Using the verse as your guide, complete this sentence.**

" ________________________ not, and you will not be judged;
________________________ not, and you will not be
________________________ ; ________________________ , and you will be forgiven."

Jesus didn't answer verbally. Instead, He ignored their question and started writing in the dirt. After a few moments, Jesus stood and asked for the person who was present who was without sin to cast the first stone.

Since the Pharisees were concerned about following the Law, Jesus reminded them by his statement that the Law required the accuser to throw the first stone (Deuteronomy 17:7).

When no one started throwing stones, Jesus started writing in the dirt again.

4 **The Bible doesn't record what Jesus wrote in the dirt. What do you think He wrote and why?**

The first time Jesus wrote He may have listed sins the accusers committed. The second time it is possible He wrote the punishment that He intended to do. If so, Jesus was following the practice of the Romans of writing a sentence before executing it.

Maybe Jesus wrote words that reminded the accusers of their own sin. It is possible Jesus wrote names and places to let them know that He knew about their adultery. Or it might have been a list of things to remind them that He knew about things they stole.

Whether it was words or drawings, the Pharisees got nervous. Convicted, they slowly began slipping away from the crowd. Jesus' actions meant that He judged the ones who were judging the woman!

Finally, only Jesus and the woman were left. Quite possibly, she still felt shame and fear. After all, the one person who was without sin and was qualified to throw the first stone remained.

5 **As believers, it is important for us to be aware of people who are shaming others by verbally judging them. What are some things you can do when you see this occurring?**

The first time Jesus spoke directly to the woman He asked her a question: where are your accusers? It is possible the woman knew from the writing in the dirt some of the reasons that the people left. Jesus wanted her to understand that He cared about her.

He immediately followed with a second question: is anyone condemning you now?

The response of the woman is significant. She replied, "No one, Lord." The use of "Lord" implied that the woman knew who Jesus was. It also implies a faith and a trust in Jesus. In other words, a change of heart occurred.

6 **Read John 3:17. Using this verse, complete the following:**

"For God did not send his ____________________ into the world to ____________________ the world, but in order that the ____________________ might be ____________________ through him."

The gospel writer doesn't record what the woman was thinking or what she felt. It is clear, however, from her response that she had a godly sorrow for her sin and a trust in Jesus. Seeing her heart, Jesus told her, "Neither do I condemn you. Go, and from now on sin no more."

Some, when first reading this story, think Jesus didn't take her adultery seriously. He did. God never overlooks our sin. And He didn't overlook this woman's sin. The love Jesus showed this woman as he came to her defense and saved her from death is the same love that He has for you.

As Christians, Jesus paid our sin debt on the cross. He took the punishment for our sin. It is through the death, burial and resurrection of Christ that we find forgiveness.

7 **We often assume that we are Christians because of where we live or the family we were born into. Being a Christian, however, means that you recognize your sin, acknowledge it, turn from it and put your faith and trust in Jesus Christ. Have you trusted Christ? If you are unsure or you know you haven't, make plans to talk with a pastor or a close Christian friend about it.**
If you have already trusted Christ, write a brief description of how it happened in your life.

The final instruction Jesus gave to this woman was to stop sinning. Jesus wasn't telling her to be perfect the rest of her life. Instead, He was reminding her that repentance means changing the way you live and think.

For this woman, it meant ending the adulterous relationship immediately. It meant serving God and following His Word. Furthermore, when someone recalled her sins, she knew she was forgiven and not standing alone when others judged her.

8 **When the woman in this story walked around town, it is possible some of the Pharisees tried to shame her again when Jesus wasn't around. Here are some of her possible responses when they did. Circle your favorites.**

- **"That was in my past, but I have a new future with Jesus."**
- **"That's true but today I am forgiven. How about you?"**
- **"I was in bondage to sexual sin but now I am free!"**
- **"Today, I am a trophy of God's grace."**

Further Study

Like the woman in John 8, King David in the Old Testament committed adultery. David poured his heart out to God in brokenness and repentance. His words in Psalm 51 illustrate how we feel about our sin when we have godly sorrow. Read Psalm 51 and make a list of the things David asked God to do.

Journal your Journey

Prayer Requests

Week Three

3

You Are Loved :
WHEN YOU FEEL UNWANTED

"When Jesus saw her, he called her over and said to her, 'Woman, you are freed from your disability."

Luke 13:12

Being unwanted is perhaps the hardest emotion to process. You wonder 'why me?' Was it something I did or something I said? If so, you plead for someone to tell you so you can correct it. Your response may or may not change another person's attitude toward you, but you feel you can correct your actions so the next person will accept you.

But there is a deeper rejection that affects the core of your self-worth. It is feeling rejected because of your race, gender, appearance or a physical challenge. In other words, it hurts when someone rejects you for reasons you cannot control or change.

1 **What would you change about your life if you could? Why do you think these changes would cause people to like and accept you more? How does culture (movies, celebrities, etc.) affect how you or others feel about your or their appearance?**

The sessions in these Bible studies examine how Jesus interacted with women and showed that He cared. There is a woman Jesus healed who is mentioned only in Luke's gospel. And it is the only place in the Bible that her type of physical challenge is mentioned (Luke 13:10-17).

Like rabbis, Jesus taught in the synagogue on the Sabbath when He could. One day, while teaching, He noticed a woman who was "bent over and could not fully straighten herself." The curvature of her spine probably meant she experienced back pain, was unable to rest at night, and limited her ability to work.

Luke, the writer of this gospel, was a doctor (Colossians 4:14). He noted that the woman suffered with this challenge for 18 years. Since life-expectancy at this time in history was much shorter than today, this woman probably developed this curvature when she was a young lady.

2 **Read I Samuel 16:7 and Proverbs 31:30. Complete these sentences to see what the Bible states about physical appearances.**

I Samuel 16:7 **"For the Lord sees not as man sees: man looks on the ____________________ appearance but the Lord looks on the ____________________."**

Proverbs 31:30 **"Charm is deceitful, and ____________________ is vain, but a woman who ____________________ the Lord is to be ____________________."**

The Bible refers to this woman as having "a spirit of infirmity" (v. 11) and being bound by Satan (v. 16). Unlike others in the New Testament, there was no indication that this woman was demon-possessed. Her appearance and physical challenges were, however, something Satan used to keep her emotionally discouraged and spiritually defeated.

It was commonly believed at the time that a disability or disease were the result of sin (see John 9:2). As a result, this woman probably wondered what she did wrong and what sins she needed to confess. She couldn't talk with a rabbi because women were forbidden to talk with them. People who could encourage her avoided her.

Nothing seemed to change until the day Jesus came to teach in the synagogue she attended.

3 **The Bible often uses the word picture of someone "bent over" as the effect sin, grief, or pain can have on a person. Why do you think these affect us in emotionally negative ways? Why do you feel God often allows these things to occur in our lives?**

When Jesus taught in the synagogue, the primary attendees were men. Women often weren't permitted inside or, if they were, they were forced to sit in the back. Jewish leaders didn't consider women as a part of the synagogue nor were they permitted to participate. Despite the way Jewish leaders treated her, the woman kept coming to the synagogue.

As Jesus taught, He noticed the woman with the curvature of the spine. Either Jesus saw her on the outside through a window or doorway or He saw her in the back. Either way, the woman didn't say anything or approach Jesus.

Instead, Jesus looked at her, and spoke clearly. He pronounced her free from her disability and from the torment Satan brought into her life.

4 **God speaks to you through the pages of the Bible. Here are some verses that express how God feels about you. Look up each one and write what the Bible says about you.**

Psalm 139:14:

Jeremiah 29:11:

Jeremiah 31:3:

Psalm 23:5:

As Jesus spoke, He lovingly touched her. Maybe Jesus put His hand on her hand or placed both hands on her shoulders to help straighten her, or maybe He put her hand in His.

In the Old Testament, touching someone or something implied it was sacred. For example, the priests touched a sacrifice before offering it to God (Exodus 29:10). The children of Israel touched or "laid hands" on the Levites to consecrate them to the priesthood (Numbers 8:9-11). Sometimes, touching was a symbol of blessing (Genesis 48:17-20).

When Jesus touched this woman, He was demonstrating how much she was loved in the eyes of God. The Pharisees wouldn't touch her because they viewed her as profane. Jesus touched her because He viewed her as sacred.

5 **Below are some ways Jesus still touches people. Circle the ones that have occurred in your life.**

- Comforted my broken heart
- Settled my anxiety
- Gave me clarity with a decision
- Made me smile
- Healed me physically
- Overwhelmed me with His love

When the woman realized she was healed – physically, emotionally, and spiritually – she praised God.

Luke was a Gentile, not a Jew. Throughout this Gospel, he noted several people who praised or glorified God. Except the Jewish shepherds at the birth of Christ, all the people Luke mentions as praising God are people shunned by the religious leaders – women, lepers, Gentiles, the sick, children, etc.

6 **Why do you think the people viewed as outcasts praised God as they encountered Jesus while the religious never did?**

The logical response for the devout Jews when they saw the woman healed was to join the celebration. They didn't. In fact, the ruler of the synagogue was upset. But he didn't express his anger to Jesus. Instead, the leader took his anger out on the people in the crowd.

The ruler or leader of the synagogue wondered why Jesus healed on the Sabbath. He could have performed the miracle on any other day of the week.
Jesus reacted by calling the ruler a hypocrite. Hypocrite originally referred to an actor in a play that changed masks to change the role he was playing. Jesus used the term to show that the leader wasn't transparent or sincere. The synagogue ruler was inconsistent.

Jesus illustrated His point by showing how the Pharisees and scribes made an exception to the law by allowing a Jew to untie an animal and lead it to water. In other words, you could help a suffering animal but not a human!

7 **In your church, how do you and others respond when someone viewed as an outcast from society becomes a Christian? How do you respond when a drug addict, a former prostitute, gang member, etc. come to your church?**

In his response to the synagogue ruler, Jesus called the healed woman a "daughter of Abraham." Since Abraham was the original person to receive the promise of God's blessings, this phrase meant this woman was a daughter of promise. She was a true child of God!

8 **This woman who was healed was called a "daughter of Abraham." Later, Zacchaeus, a tax collector who also was an outcast, was called a "son of Abraham" (Luke 19:9). How do they compare to the rich man in Luke 16:19-31? Why did the rich man think that he was a child of God (or a son of Abraham) when he wasn't? What makes the difference?**

This woman is a picture of everyone's spiritual condition. Satan and sin have everyone "bent over" and unable to straighten their lives. You are unable to change yourself. But Jesus loves you and speaks to you. He comes to you today through the voice of the Holy Spirit. Like this woman, by simple faith you can be delivered from the power of sin.

Further Study

Christians often overreact to Satan by giving him too much attention or ignoring him. A Biblical understanding of the role of Satan and his inferiority to our Heavenly Father is essential. To understand the way Satan often uses suffering to change our commitment to Christ, read the first two chapters of Job. What do you discover about pain? Why does God permit it? How are Satan's powers limited? How are you encouraged when you remember that your Heavenly Father is in control?

Journal your Journey

Prayer Requests

Week Four

4

You Are Loved :
WHEN YOU FEEL SHAME

"And he said to her, 'Daughter, your faith has made you well; go in peace, and be healed of your disease.'"

Mark 5:34

Nothing destroys self-worth more than shame. It affects how we act around people, how we feel about ourselves, and how we approach life. It makes us feel unwanted and unloved.

Shame is rooted in the belief that we are not good enough or we fail to measure up to a minimum standard. We fear being exposed and, in turn, rejected.

Society often reinforces our shame. Comments or questions can be painful, especially in the presence of others. When people remind us that we aren't as educated, as attractive, or as desirable as someone else, shame makes us want to run and hide.

1 **Think about the following questions that people often are asked. How do you think each person feels when they hear these questions?**

Aren't you divorced?

Didn't you fail college?

Isn't your father an alcoholic?

Isn't your son in prison?

Jesus once encountered a woman filled with shame. Shame kept her from approaching Jesus directly. As a person declared unclean, she knew Jesus would never touch her. She, however, thought she might be healed if she touched Jesus without anyone knowing.

She waited for the perfect moment. The opportunity came when a ruler of a Jewish synagogue, desperate to save the life of his only child, pleaded with Jesus to come to his home and heal his daughter. This was the first time a Jewish leader showed Jesus respect. Because of its rarity, a large crowd gathered to see what Jesus would do.

As the crowd started walking toward his home, an unnamed woman with "a discharge of blood" for 12 years quietly approached Jesus from behind. She believed that He could heal her, but shame forced her to quietly approach Jesus from behind.

2 **Read Mark 5:25-26. List three reasons why you think this woman was too embarrassed to ask Jesus for help.**

1. ______________________________

2. ______________________________

3. ______________________________

The hemorrhage affected her quality of life. It left her weak and unhealthy. To prevent the spread of blood-borne diseases, the Jews had strict rules. The Law set a hygiene code that forbid the woman from being around other people or going near the Temple area (Leviticus 15:19-31).

The woman was treated socially the same as a leper. Whoever or whatever she touched was ceremonially unclean. Any person she touched must immediately bathe and change clothes. People avoided her.

3 **Review Mark 5:25-26 and read Matthew 9:20-22. This woman was affected physically, socially, spiritually and financially. Which of these caused her shame? If you were her, how do you think you would feel?**

Physically

Socially

Spiritually

Financially

The woman was desperate. She had lost everything – money, self-worth, and hope. What she desired most was hope, any hope that tomorrow might be better than today. Jesus offered her that hope. Shame told her to stay away but love drew her to Jesus.

4 **People with shame often avoid church services or church activities because they fear rejection. What are some ways that you/your church can make church approachable for people dealing with shame?**

The woman approached Jesus from behind. While walking, everyone would be facing forward. If she could touch Him quickly, no one would rebuke her.

It isn't clear what part of Jesus' clothing she touched. Traditionally, most people think she bent over, possibly hiding her face, and touched the hem near His ankle. Some scholars believe that it was probably one of the four tassels that every Jew wore on the four corners of His square, outer robe. These tassels reminded the Jew of the Law of God (Numbers 15:38).

5 **Of the following, put a circle around the actions you/your church can do to make people feel loved/wanted and a box around the ones that don't.**

Offering free food	Staring at people
Refusing to greet visitors	Telling people what a blessing they are
Inviting people to a fellowship	Asking personal questions

When the woman touched the garment of Jesus, she instantly was healed. By the Law, her touch made Jesus unclean. But grace didn't make Jesus unclean. It made her clean.

She knew she was healed, and she probably thought of leaving immediately. Jesus, however, stopped walking and asked, "Who touched my garments?" As God, Jesus knew who touched Him. He asked for her benefit. He wanted her to confront her shame, step forward and forever be freed from it.

The disciples, led by Peter (Luke 8:45), reminded Jesus that many people were touching him. One, however, was different. One touch came with a faith in His healing power.

Fear and shame run together. It is no surprise that fear gripped this woman. For starters, a woman wasn't allowed to speak in the presence of men, especially a Rabbi. By coming forward, she expected rejection, ridicule, and additional shame to come from Jesus.

6 **People dealing with shame often need encouragement and reassurance. Who is someone you know who needs encouragement especially because their heart is hurting as a result of something beyond their control? How can you help?**

____

____

____

____

____

____

____

When she told Jesus "the whole truth," Jesus responded with the most powerful, kind and compassionate words that she could have imagined.

7 **Complete the words Jesus spoke to the woman after she told Him about her situation and what had happened.**

"And he said to her, "____________________, your ____________________ has made you well; go in ____________________ , and be healed of your ____________________ ." (Mark 5:34)

When Jesus called the woman "daughter," He meant she was a daughter of Israel. It wasn't confirming her Jewish heritage but restoring her to all the privileges she had before getting sick. It was an affectionate term, much like a loving Father would say to his daughter. After 12 years of being excluded, Jesus said that she was now included.

Jesus commended her faith. Before she approached Jesus, she accepted who He was and believed His words.
Then Jesus looked at her and gave a traditional farewell. He told her to "go in peace." Peace was a Hebrew concept of Shalom, a profound experience of well-being that resulted from salvation. It included wholeness, blessings, and security. It was God's approval of her healing.

8 **Think of the shame that you may feel at times. Now review the four things this woman did that set her free. What do you need to do to be free from your shame?**

She acknowledged the shame she felt. I need to acknowledge that I feel shame because of ________________________.

She touched Jesus. I need to touch Jesus by ______________________ .

She was transparent about her feelings. I need to start processing my feelings by ____________________________ .

She accepted what Jesus said about her and rejected what others said. I need to accept that Jesus said I am ______________________ .

The Bible doesn't record how the healed woman responded. Jesus immediately continued onto Jairus' house. It is possible she visited the Temple area, talked with people, and held her head high.

The woman who was told to stay away, now could lead a parade of worshipers.

The woman who wasn't invited to visit in a home, now could visit all her relatives.

The woman who didn't feel loved because of her shame, met perfect love and her shame went away.

For this woman, Jesus restored what shame took away.

Shame took her joy, but Jesus put a song in her heart!

Further Study

Like the woman with the issue of blood, shame often comes from things we cannot control. It might be our appearance, our financial status, or our neighborhood. Other times it comes from what others do (our rebellious child or an unfaithful spouse). But there is a third source of shame that comes from sins we commit. Read Matthew 26:30-35, Luke 22:54-62 and Matthew 26:69-75 about Peter's three denials of Jesus. What caused Peter to think that he would never deny Christ? How was his shame connected to his boasting? How did Peter respond when he realized what he had done? How does Romans 8:1 apply to anyone who is repentant about their sin but still embarrassed by it?

Journal your Journey

Prayer Requests

Week Five

5

You Are Loved :
WHEN RELATIONSHIPS FAIL

"Jesus said to her, 'Everyone who drinks of this water will be thirsty again, but whoever drinks of the water that I will give him will never be thirsty again."

Mark 5:34

You could not contain your excitement when you met the new lady at work. Over time, your friendship grew, and you started sharing your deepest thoughts and secrets. Finally, someone you enjoyed having as your friend, who shared the same interests and was someone who seemed to care about you.

Then, a new position opened at work. Everyone thought you would get the job. But you didn't. You later learned that your "friend" shared confidential information and opinions that kept you from getting the job.

Friendships aren't the only relationships that fail. You married the person that you thought was your dream spouse only to watch your dream marriage turn into a nightmare. Maybe a sibling or a neighbor refuses to speak to you because of a disagreement you had.

Jesus once interacted with a woman who experienced several failed relationships. Her story, recorded in John chapter 4, began when Jesus traveled from Judea to Galilee. Although the road through Samaria was the quickest route, most Jews avoided it because they didn't want to interact with the Samaritans.

1 **People often avoid other people. Circle some of the reasons you have found that cause some people to avoid others.**

Political	Past Conflicts	Religious
Personality	Racial	Financial
Lifestyle	Poverty	Jealousy

Samaritans were a mixed race. Years earlier, when the Assyrians conquered the northern kingdom of Israel, they deported most of the Israelites and brought captives from other places to settle there. The foreigners brought their own pagan religions with them. Before long, they intermarried and created their own religious beliefs.

By the time of Jesus, the Jews hated the Samaritans. The Jews believed that associating with a Samaritan dishonored God. But Jesus wasn't about pushing perceived enemies away. Instead, He engaged in a relationship with them.

2 **Read I John 4:8. What does the Bible say about individuals who hate others? Fill in the blanks to find out.**

"Anyone who does not ____________________ does not know __________________________, because God is ____________________."

Jesus arrived at a small village called Sychar. He sat down near a well Jacob dug while the disciples went into town to buy food. It was about 6:00 in the evening, about the time that the women came to get water from the well.

The woman recognized Jesus as a Jew and assumed that He would not speak to her. No Jew, especially a Rabbi, would talk to a woman alone in public in Jerusalem, much less a Samaritan woman!

3 **The Samaritan woman expected Jesus to ignore her. When someone is different from you, how do they expect you to respond to them? How do they expect your church to respond? If there is a negative perception, what can you do to change it?**

She intended to get the water and leave quietly. But Jesus requested a drink of water. His request surprised her. Speaking to her was one thing, but no Jew would drink water from a water pot owned by a Samaritan and certainly not from a cup that a Samaritan used!
The woman's response was to make sure Jesus understood that she was a Samaritan and to clarify, at least to herself, that He was a Jew. She asked Jesus a question, wondering why a Jew would ask a Samaritan for a drink of water.

Jesus didn't answer her question directly. Instead, He told the Samaritan woman that if she knew who He was, she would ask Him for a drink of living water.

The Samaritan woman knew that there were two different ways to get water. One way was to obtain rainwater as it fell and the other was to find a well with a spring in the bottom. This woman thought that the living water Jesus referenced referred to the water in the well. But she was confused on how Jesus could offer it since He didn't have anything to lower into the well to draw the water.

Maybe, she thought, Jesus had a better well nearby. If so, that meant He was better or greater than Jacob. Like the Jews, the Samaritans traced their heritage to Jacob. The Samaritans believed that they were descendants of Joseph. So, she asked Jesus two questions: How was he going to draw water without? Are you greater than Jacob?

Jesus again ignored her question and focused her attention on the water that He offered. Jesus explained it was a bubbling stream that was the source of eternal life. The response the woman at the well gave indicates that she is seeking something more.

4 **Jesus often used common things known to his hearers to illustrate who He was. Read the following scriptures and note what Jesus used.**

John 6:35 ______________________________

____

____

John 8:12 ______________________________

____

____

John 10:1 ______________________________

____

____

John 10:9 ______________________________

____

____

John 15:1 ______________________________

____

____

Jesus knew that this woman needed to understand her spiritual need and how she could receive living water. But the woman needed to see it instead of Jesus lecturing her.

Again, Jesus ignored her question. He then asked the woman to go get her husband. The Samaritan society didn't approve of a man talking to a woman without her husband present. Although the woman probably thought Jesus was following her cultural practices, Jesus was causing her to see the need of a new relationship.

The woman admitted that she wasn't married. Jesus, to illustrate His all-knowing deity, confirmed her statement and added that she was living with a man who wasn't her husband. Jesus also revealed that she had five previous husbands.

To be fair, it is possible that some of her previous husbands died. The tone of Jesus' words, however, imply five divorces. The woman talking with Jesus longed to be loved but failed to find it in her relationships.

Feeling uncomfortable with the knowledge Jesus had, the woman tried to change the subject. Jesus, she admitted, apparently was a prophet since He knew about her marriages. Maybe, she thought, He could answer a religious question: where was the proper place to worship God?

The Jews believed Jerusalem was the only place worship could occur. The Samaritans, however, weren't allowed in Jerusalem. They remembered the Old Testament teaching that Mount Gerizim was a place of blessing (Deuteronomy 11:29; 27:12).

They reasoned, therefore, that it was the correct place to worship. It happened to conveniently be in the area where the Samaritans lived and where no Jew would go.

Again, Jesus refused to debate religious questions. Worship was not about a place but about being open and honest with God.

5 **Debates about worship continue today. What do the words of Jesus in John 4:23-24 teach about real worship?**

Both the Jews and the Samaritans focused on places and methods of worship. For Jesus, real worship came from the heart. God is more concerned with the sincerity of our praise than the place of worship. That is why Jesus reminded the woman that God is a Spirit that isn't limited to one place or to one race of people. He was a personal God who cared about individuals.

6 **The New Testament describes God in four different ways. Read each verse and write how God is described. What do you think each description means?**

John 4:24

I John 1:5

I John 4:8 ______________________________

____

____

Hebrews 12:29 ______________________________

____

Unlike the Jews who believed all the Old Testament, the Samaritans only accepted the first five books of the Bible as divinely inspired. But, like the Jews, they looked for the Messiah. Samaritans believed Deuteronomy 18:15-22 taught that the one way to know the Messiah was His ability to reveal things that came true.

The woman, knowing what she was taught, started to sense Jesus might be the Messiah. Then, Jesus directly admitted that He was the promised Messiah.

During their conversation, the woman who came to draw water moved from acknowledging Jesus as a Jew, to asking if He was greater than Jacob, to admitting He was a prophet, to recognizing that Jesus was the promised Messiah.

The woman's reaction demonstrates how the truth of the gospel affects people. First, she left her water jar at the well. The Greek word used for "left" didn't mean that she forgot it. It was an intentional act. She probably left it so Jesus and the disciples could drink. She didn't mind. Sure, water jars were valuable possessions, but Jesus was something better.

Then, she rushed into town to tell everyone about the man at the well. Her message to the residents of Sychar was simple and straightforward. There was a man at the well who told her things that only she knew. Could this man be the Messiah?

The leaders of the city normally wouldn't believe a woman. Something about her words, however, interested them. Maybe it was her excitement or the smile on her face. Maybe it was her passion. Or maybe because it was obvious that she had found the love she sought in relationships.

Whatever it was, the people came to the well. The ability of a man to tell hidden secrets interested them. After they heard and met Jesus, many of the Samaritans believed in Christ.

Later, the citizens of Sychar admitted that they came because of what the woman said but they believed because of what Jesus said (John 4:42). They, too, found in Jesus what they could not find in a relationship with another person.

Further Study

Personal accounts of a person meeting Christ is a powerful tool used by the Holy Spirit to bring conviction in the hearts of unbelievers. Read these three testimonies in the New Testament that God used to change a heart: (1) Philip's words to Nathanael (John 1:43-51), (2) Stephen's words before the high priest (Acts 7:1-60), and (3) Acts 26:1-23. What or who was the focus of their words? Who did their words affect? How can you share your personal story about meeting Jesus?

Journal your Journey

Prayer Requests

Week Six

6

You Are Loved : WHEN SATAN HAS A STRONGHOLD ON A CHILD

"Then Jesus answered her, 'O woman, great is your faith! Be it done for you as you desire.' And her daughter was healed instantly."

Matthew 15:28

Nothing grieves like the heart of a parent with a rebellious child or one ensnared by an addiction. We cry. We pray and ask God for their deliverance. We plead with our children to change. We finally realize that Satan and sin has a stronghold in their life, and only the power of the Holy Spirit can change their life.

1 **Do you have a child that sin is destroying? Write a prayer specifically asking God to work in the life of your child. Or you might want to write a prayer for a grandchild, another relative or a friend's child.**

Matthew and Mark recorded in their gospels (Matthew 15:21-28 and Mark 7:24-30) the story of a woman desperate for her daughter to be set free from demon possession. She wasn't like the other women Jesus encountered in His ministry. She was a Gentile who lived outside of Palestine. By any standard of her day, there was no reason for Jesus to care about her or her daughter.

Jesus' ministry occurred mainly in the area around the Sea of Galilee. He traveled to nearby areas and Jerusalem occasionally but not often.

This event, however, occurred in the region known as Tyre and Sidon. The area was north of Galilee, about 40 miles from Capernaum. In the Old Testament, David and Solomon made an alliance with the kings of Tyre and through this alliance, Baal worship was introduced to the Israelites (Isaiah 23).

Jesus came here because He wanted time to rest and to prepare His disciples for the days after His resurrection. Crowds in Palestine prevented Him from resting or teaching in private. Someone always wanted His attention. Jesus left Palestine and came to Tyre and Sidon for that purpose.

The people who lived in Tyre and Sidon were the bitter enemies of the Jews. The residents were financially successful, often paying more for food in Palestine than the Jews could afford. Many of the Jews suffered because of their success.

When Jesus arrived, He was unable to hide. News about His miracles already reached the area. People knew who He was and gathered to see and hear Him.

One woman was desperate to see Jesus. Matthew described her as a Canaanite (Matthew 15:22). Mark noted that she was a Gentile and a Syrophoenician by birth (Mark 7:26). As a Canaanite, her ancestors caused many of the problems Joshua and the Israelites faced when they entered the promised land. She is identified as a Syrophoenician. This meant she was a native of Phoenicia, a province of Syria. She had a pagan background and little understanding of God. Since nothing was mentioned about her husband, she may have been a widow.

2 **Of all the miracles Jesus did, many involved women. The Syrophoenician woman is one. Read the account of these women and note what emotions or feelings they probably shared with this woman.**

The grieving widow (Luke 7:11-17)

Mary and Martha (John 11:17-44)

The woman addressed Jesus as "Lord" and "Son of David" (Matthew 15:22). These phrases indicated that this pagan woman was a believer in Jesus as one sent by God. She knew that He was the promised Messiah of the Jews.

If you put the ministry in chronological order, this woman was the first person since John the Baptist to acknowledge the deity of Christ. Because she knew Jesus was God, she believed that He could help her daughter.
She told Jesus that a demon possessed her child, a unique perception for someone with a pagan background, and pleaded for His help. Jesus didn't acknowledge her or her words. It isn't clear why, but it is possible Jesus wanted to use the occasion to teach His disciples about the inclusion of the Gentiles in the plan of God, something that would be vital for them to understand after His ascension.

When Jesus didn't respond to her, the disciples pleaded for Him to send her away. The disciples weren't concerned about her daughter. They just didn't want to be bothered about it. Maybe they thought learning from Jesus was more important than this woman or her demon-possessed child. The pain of a parent with a wayward child increases when Christians don't seem to care.

3 **Circle the ways Christians can convey that they are concerned about people with a stronghold in their life or the lives of their family.**

Praying for them	Gossiping about them
Avoiding them	Finding ways to minister to them
Listening	Telling them to go away

Just as Jesus didn't respond to the woman's comment, neither did He address the request of the disciples to send her away. He, instead, told them that He was sent to the "lost sheep of the house of Israel." The disciples probably took that phrase to mean that this woman, as a Gentile, didn't deserve help. That would have been a normal response from a Jewish man.

Jesus was sowing the thoughts that salvation was for all people, not just the Jews. As the disciples would later discover, Jesus brought the message of salvation first to the Jews, but they rejected Him. Now the gospel is open to everyone, Jew or Gentile.

4 **Complete these verses using John 1:11-12:**

"He came to his own, and his own ______________________ did not ______________________ him. But to ______________________ who did receive him, who ______________________ in his ______________________, he gave the ______________________ to become ______________________ of God."

The woman refused to go away. She was desperate. The second time (Matt. 15:25), she changed her plea from acknowledging who He was ("Lord" and "Son of David") with an unspoken request to help her daughter, to "Lord, help me."

Often the change that needs to come in the life of a child begins with healing the hurt in the heart of the parent. Jesus certainly felt the pain of this woman's heart.

The response of Jesus to her seems cruel, but Jesus knew what He was going to do. His response probably had the disciples in mind.

Jesus said that it wasn't right to give food meant for children to dogs. Jesus was comparing the Gentiles to dogs. In the minds of the disciples, the Gentiles weren't worthy of salvation.

The woman pleaded by noting in the word picture Jesus used, that people gave at least crumbs to dogs. The word translated "dogs" referred to house puppies or pets. It implied that dogs received some compassion when they were hurting.

It is easy for believers to see some people as undeserving of the gospel or, at least, that they aren't interested. Read this list of people, and if someone comes to your mind, pray for them and their salvation.

Person in prison

Prostitute

Drug Addict

Atheist

Member of non-Christian religion

Person who betrayed/stole from you

The one person in this story who knew love was the possessed child. A mother who would go to the lengths she did demonstrates that love never stops caring. Now, the mother was able to experience love too when Jesus honored her request.

As the disciples were watching and listening, Jesus told the woman she had great faith. Only twice did Jesus tell someone that they had great faith – this woman and the centurion whose servant Jesus healed (Luke 7:1-10). Both were Gentiles, not Jews. And neither came from a religious background. They were hurting, and Jesus was their answer.

By contrast, Jesus never told His disciples that they possessed great faith. Faith was something hard for the disciples to learn.

But when Jesus saw her faith, He answered her prayer. Her daughter was healed instantly. The demon left her as Jesus spoke.

After Jesus spoke, the woman verified her faith by going home. She took Jesus at His word. Mark noted that when the woman arrived home, she "found the child lying in bed and the demon gone."

Hurting parents often wonder why Jesus doesn't deliver their child. They wonder why the addictions continue or why their child continues to make wrong choices.

Although this story centers solely on the mother, we don't know what was happening in the life of the child. Demonic strongholds are powerful and can only be broken when a child is willing and ready for God to break those chains of bondage.

But this story illustrates that struggling parents are not alone. They may think that God doesn't hear their prayers and their cries for help, but he does.

5. Review the prayer you wrote early in this study. Now, rewrite your prayer telling God exactly how you feel. Be specific about your hurts and struggles. Tell the Lord what you want Him to do in your life and in the life of your child. After writing the prayer, ask God to speak to you about the ways He can use you to bring healing into the life of your child. Again, you may want to pray for a grandchild, a friend's child or another relative.

Further Study

Read Luke 15:11-20. Make a list of the things that the father of the prodigal son did and did not do. Make another list of the things the father said and did not say. Finally, write how you think the father felt when his son left, while he was gone, and when he returned.

As a parent with a child that isn't serving the Lord, you might be encouraged by Reaching Your Prodigal: What Did I Do Wrong? What Do I Do Now? by Phil Waldrep. It is available at www.philwaldrep.org or where most books are sold.

Journal your Journey

Prayer Requests

Week Seven

7

You Are Loved :
WHEN YOU LOSE SOMEONE YOU LOVE

"And when the Lord saw her, he had compassion on her and said to her, 'Do not weep.'"

Luke 7:13

When someone you love dies, your heart hurts. The greater your love and the closer the person was to you, the greater the pain will be. It leaves a void in your life, a hole in your heart. You wonder how you can live another day. And you start to assume that you will never be happy again.

While on earth, Jesus raised three different people from the dead, two men and one girl. All three times, His actions comforted and ministered primarily to women.

For example, when Jesus raised the daughter of Jairus (Luke 8:49-56), He included her mother in the room when the miracle occurred.

When Jesus raised Lazarus from the dead, He wept with his sisters, Mary and Martha, before performing the miracle (John 8:1-44).

And when Jesus raised the widow's son (Luke 7:11-17), the blessing was greater than the widow could ever imagine.

1 In the culture of Jesus' day, men did not value women. How do you think Jairus' wife, Mary and Martha, and the widow felt after their loved ones were brought back to life?

The story of the widow's son being raised from the dead is found only in the Gospel of Luke (Luke 7:11-17). It demonstrates how our grief touches the heart of God when someone we love dies.

When Luke wrote about the life of Jesus, he often paired events together. Luke 7 opens with Jesus healing the servant of a centurion, a Roman officer who helped the Jewish community. Luke immediately follows with the story of the widow and her deceased son.

Jesus and His disciples were approaching Nain, slightly over 20 miles from Capernaum and approximately six miles from Nazareth. This is the only place in the Bible that Nain is mentioned.

As they neared the city's gate, they saw a funeral procession coming out of the city. Family and friends were going to the cemetery to bury a young man, the only son of a widow.

2 **Imagine you were the widow who lost her only son. Circle the emotions the widow probably had as she walked to the cemetery. Then, draw a square around three emotions you experienced the last time you lost someone you loved.**

Disbelief	Fear	Blame
Hopelessness	Anger	Uncertainty
Guilt	Frustration	Sadness

It was the custom for family members of a Jew who died to tear their garments as a sign of mourning. Others would come and anoint the body and wrap it in a garment as preparation for burial. The body wasn't placed in a casket but on a flat board to be carried to a cemetery outside of town.

Because Jews were buried on the same day they died, family and friends, along with professional mourners, would gather at the home. Late in the afternoon, a procession would form. With the body in the front, men went first, followed by women.

The procession went through town and out the city's gate. In ancient times, a city's gate was very important. If the city had walls, the gate was the point of entry. But many cities didn't have walls. They had a decorative gate, much like modern cities have at the entrance of town.

Political and business leaders often conducted business by the gate. Anything of significance happened here.

As the procession exited the gate, they encountered Jesus and his disciples entering. It wasn't a coincidence. Jesus worked on a divine timetable. A procession of death was encountering a procession of life.

3 **Death and life are often a picture of salvation. Using John 5:24, complete this verse:**

"Truly, truly, I say to you, whoever ____________________ my word and ____________________ him who sent me has ____________________ life. He does not come into judgment, but has passed from ____________________ to life."

Normally, someone seeing a funeral procession would step to the side and let them pass. But Jesus didn't. Instead, He stopped the procession.

Jesus saw the widow and had compassion. He and His disciples probably knew she was a widow by no father being with the men or a husband walking with her. Jesus felt and shared her grief.

As a widow losing her only son, her future would be a financial hardship. Women had few opportunities to earn money, and most widows eventually had to beg for food.

Jesus first told her, "Do not weep." This statement was in contrast with His actions when Lazarus died (John 11:35). Jesus didn't condemn her tears or scold her for crying. His words were a message of hope.

It is natural to cry when someone dies. God sees and feels our grief. Read the following verses and note what God promises to do with our tears.

Psalm 56:8

Revelation 21:4

After Jesus spoke to the woman, He touched the wooden plank that was holding the body. No one expected a Jewish rabbi to touch anything associated with death. According to the Law, touching a dead body or anything associated with a dead body made a person unclean for seven days (Numbers 19:11,16).

Once the procession stopped, Jesus spoke to the dead man. He instructed him to arise.

To everyone's surprise, the young man sat up. And to confirm the young man really was alive, he began to speak. Luke doesn't record what the young man said, or how he got off the plank. Maybe the pallbearers put the plank on the ground for everyone to see and hear the resurrected man more clearly.

Luke added one unique detail. He said that Jesus gave the man to his mother. Throughout the story, Jesus focused on the widow and her grief. His ministry was to her.

4 **Again, imagine you were this mother. How do you think this event affected her relationships with the following? After noting it, how should the hope of a future resurrection affect our relationships now?**

Her son ______________________________

____

Her family/friends ______________________________

____

Jesus ______________________________

____

The response to Jesus after the miracle wasn't a surprise. First, fear seized them. It was an emotional reaction because they sensed Jesus was truly from God. They realized that anyone who could raise the dead had incredible power.

Second, they glorified God. The focus of everyone in the procession was Jesus, not the resurrected man or the mother.

Finally, the people said that a prophet had arisen among them and that God had visited them. Since the people didn't understand that Jesus was the Messiah, the only logical reaction was to call Him a prophet. The people knew that the Old Testament prophets Elijah and Elisha raised the dead, so it was natural to think that Jesus must be a prophet.

Others realized that He was more than a prophet. They saw Him, or at least His actions, as a visitation from God. And for those who knew about Him, resurrecting the man affirmed His deity.

While Jesus healed many people, He only raised three from the dead. Resurrecting a dead person, something He did only late in his earthly ministry, validated his Messiahship. Immediately following this event, Jesus referred to it when messengers came from John the Baptist and asked Jesus if He was the Messiah (Luke 7:18-24).

5 **It is common for people to think only the godliest receive miracles. Jesus said that the greatest man born was John the Baptist (Luke 7:28). Yet, John the Baptist was killed (Mark 6:14-29). Why do you think Jesus resurrected a few but not others? Why do you think He didn't resurrect John the Baptist?**

After His resurrection, Jesus ascended to Heaven. He gave a promise before He departed that He would return (John 14:1-4). Paul added that the return of Christ will result in every Christian being resurrected from the dead.

6 **Use I Thessalonians 4:16 to complete the following:**

"For the Lord himself shall descend from ______________ with a cry of command, with the voice of an ______________, and with the sound of the ______________ of God. And the ______________ in Christ will ______________ ______________ first."

When you lose someone you love, it isn't a permanent goodbye. For every believer, death is not final. When we lose someone we love, God still loves us and feels our grief.

Further Study

The raising of the widow's son is very similar to Elijah raising a widow's son back to life. Read the account in I Kings 17:17-24. How is the story similar? How is it different? How do the emotions of the widow (anger toward Elijah, etc.) reflect the emotions you felt when you lost someone? Why do you think God allowed Elijah to perform this miracle?

Journal your Journey

Prayer Requests

Week Eight

8

You Are Loved :
WHEN ALL HOPE IS LOST

"Jesus said to her, 'Mary.' She turned and said to him in Aramaic, 'Rabboni!" (which means Teacher)

John 20:16

Someone wrote many years ago that a person could live without food for 40 days, three days without water, eight minutes without air but only one second without hope.

When the Apostle Paul wrote I Corinthians 13, a story often referred to as the love chapter in the Bible, he noted the three things essential in the Christian life were faith, hope and love. Believers often talk about the importance of faith and love but rarely about hope.

The early Christians understood the role hope played in their lives. Persecution caused them to long for the return of Christ and the promise of Heaven. Paul often called it the blessed hope (Titus 2:13).

Hope is knowing that the future is better than today. It is knowing that the pain of the moment will cease, and a greater joy will come. As the Psalmist wrote in Psalm 30:5, "Weeping may tarry for the night, but joy comes in the morning."

1 Everyone has a moment when they feel a situation or life is hopeless. It might be after a divorce, a child is arrested, your job is terminated, or someone dies. Think of a time when you felt hopeless. Write what you felt here. Why did you feel that way? What gave you hope that life would get better?

There is a woman in the New Testament who felt hopeless. Her name was Mary Magdalene. Unlike our modern times, that wasn't her first and last name. It was a short version for Mary of Magdala. Since many Jewish women were named Mary, often people identified which Mary they meant by telling us their hometown.

Magdala means tower or fortress. It probably identified a city or community on the western short of the Sea of Galilee. It probably got its name because of a tower or fortress nearby.

Mary Magdalene first appears in Luke 8:1-3. She is listed among a group of women who were traveling with Jesus and were financially supporting His work. Both Luke and Mark noted that she had been possessed by seven demons (Mark 16:9/Luke 8:2). Although the Bible doesn't record the event, it is safe to assume that Jesus set her free.

It is interesting to note, however, that she is mentioned most during the death and resurrection of Jesus. She watched the crucifixion (Matthew 27:55-56). She was present when Joseph from Arimathea placed Jesus' body in the tomb (Matthew 27:57-61). For her, that was the day she lost hope.

2 **What does Psalm 42:11 tell us to do when we feel hopeless? Complete the verse by filling in the blanks to find out.**

"Why are you ____________ down, O my soul, and why are you in ____________ turmoil within me? ____________ in God, for I shall again ____________ him, my ____________ and my God." Psalm 42:11

Mary Magdalene put her hope in God when she met Jesus. The seven demons that possessed her left. She was free. She wanted to spend her life knowing more about God and His Son.

Like others, Mary Magdalene didn't expect the crucifixion. She watched Him die, and she watched as His body was put into a tomb. Now she had to process her grief and the feelings of hopelessness for the future.

On the Sabbath Day, as the Law required, she rested. That night, three women (Mary Magdalene, another Mary, and Salome) decided to return to the tomb and rewrap the body of Jesus with additional spices (Mark 16:1). It was a common practice for women to go to a tomb, have someone move the stone that covered the entrance, and put spices on the body. But when they arrived, the tomb was empty. While they were on their way to the tomb is probably when the resurrection occurred, and the stone was rolled from the entrance.

Mark noted that an angel appeared to the women and announced the resurrection of Christ (Mark 16:5-6). He also instructed them to go and tell His disciple in the following verse.

The Gospel of John recorded that Mary Magdalene immediately told Peter and John what she found. She thought that the Roman authorities had moved the body of Jesus. Peter and John, then, ran to the tomb. John realized that Jesus was alive. Peter didn't.

Mary Magdalene stayed after Peter and John left. She again entered the tomb. For a second time, an angel spoke to her. Mary Magdalene didn't believe that Jesus was alive. She even told the angel that she was crying because she didn't know where the body of Jesus was.

3 **Mary Magdalene saw and heard an angel report the resurrection of Jesus. Later, an angel would ask her why she was crying (John 20:11-13). Mary Magdalene continued to believe that the body was stolen. Why do you think Mary Magdalene doubted the angels? Why do you think we often doubt when God has spoken to us through His word?**

Mary Magdalene cried because she couldn't see a future without Jesus in it. No one loved her like Jesus. She devoted her life to helping Him share His message of love and forgiveness. Now, what would she do?

Her emotions clouded reality. Angels told her that Jesus was alive, but that seemed impossible. Instead of listening to the angels, she chose to keep wondering where the body of Jesus was.

Everyone handles grief differently. Peter, John and Mary Magdalene all were grieving the death of Jesus. On a scale of 1 to 10 (1 being not at all, and 10 being absolutely), how do you use these actions to handle grief?

Crying	1	2	3	4	5	6	7	8	9	10
Talking	1	2	3	4	5	6	7	8	9	10
Writing Thoughts	1	2	3	4	5	6	7	8	9	10
Counseling	1	2	3	4	5	6	7	8	9	10

After she spoke to the angel, she turned and saw someone standing behind her. It was Jesus, but she didn't recognize Him. Maybe her tears blurred her vision. Or maybe her disbelief in the resurrection didn't allow her to accept that it was Jesus.

Jesus called her "woman" and asked her two questions: why are you weeping? And who are you seeking? Calling Mary Magdalene "woman" was not impolite or unkind. It was a common greeting for a man to use when He didn't know a woman's name. It would be the modern equivalent of calling a woman "ma'am."

The two questions Jesus asked were intended to focus her attention onto Jesus as the promised Messiah. One of the questions repeated what the angel asked Mary Magdalene moments earlier.

Mary Magdalene didn't recognize the resurrected body of Jesus nor did she recognize His voice. She assumed that the person who spoke was a gardener who cared for that area. She called him "Sir," a polite greeting in hopes that he would tell her where the body of Jesus was.

Hopelessness causes deep emotions to surface. And emotions can cause us to reject a truth, make poor judgments, or say things that we later regret. Circle the things people often do when they are feeling hopeless and emotional about a situation in their lives.

Scream at people	Smile	Get angry
Pray for people	Make bad choices	Go to church
Withdraw from people	Act like nothing is wrong	Seek revenge

Jesus felt the hurt in Mary Magdalene's heart. Instead of telling her that He was alive, Jesus simply called her name, "Mary." Unlike the other words Jesus uttered, hearing her name had a special effect. She immediately recognized Jesus.

Mary Magdalene cried out, "Rabboni." John noted that she spoke in Aramaic and translated the word as teacher. Historians note that this word was never used to refer to a human rabbi. It was her expression of her faith in the deity and Lordship of Jesus.

Mary Magdalene grabbed his feet and held them tightly. Jesus kindly told her not to cling to Him. In her mind, she probably thought that she would never let Jesus out of her sight again! Mary Magdalene may have felt the presence of Jesus much like Peter, James and John did on the Mount of Transfiguration (Mark 9:2-13).

Mary Magdalene was the first person to see Jesus after His resurrection. Jesus told her to go and report His appearance to the disciples. The Jewish culture didn't permit a woman to give testimony in court. Jewish men didn't consider them as credible witnesses. Jesus, however, first gave Mary Magdalene and the other women the responsibility to report the resurrection.

When Jesus told Mary Magdalene to report their encounter, Jesus didn't call His followers disciples. He called them "brothers." After the resurrection, a new and deeper relationship existed between Jesus and His followers.

As believers, Jesus instructed us to share the gospel with people who don't know Christ. Many of these people feel hopeless and Christians know the gospel brings hope. List here the names of four people who you know aren't believers. Take a moment to pray for them and ask God to give you a chance to share the gospel with them.

1. ______________________________

2. ______________________________

3. ______________________________

4. ______________________________

Throughout the Gospels, Jesus interacted with women like few others did. He valued them. He listened to them and appreciated them. Today, Jesus still values women because He loves them with an everlasting love.

Further Study

Hopelessness can happen whenever a major change occurs in our lives. Our plans and vision for the future are shattered. In the Old Testament, Job should have been a hopeless man. He wondered why things happened to him, but he never lost his faith in God. Read the first two chapters and the last chapter of Job. What did he lose? Why did he lose it? What did he learn about God through his pain? How did God bless him again?

Journal your Journey

Prayer Requests

Additional Notes